The GigAntic Little Hero

A Story about Perseverance

Written and Illustrated by
Matt Whitlock

Equipping Kids for Life

A Faith Parenting Guide can be found on page 32.

Faith Kids® is an imprint of
Cook Communications Ministries, Colorado Springs, CO 80918
Cook Communications, Paris, Ontario
Kingsway Communications, Eastbourne, England

THE GIGANTIC LITTLE HERO
© 2001 by Matthew Whitlock for text and illustrations.

Edited by Jeannie Harmon
Designed by Yaye Design

First printing, 2001
Printed in Singapore
04 03 02 01 00   5 4 3 2 1

Library of Congress Cataloging-in-Publication Data

ISBN 0-7814-3517-X

Dedicated to:
Jenny
and to the memory of
Charles M. Schulz (1922-2000)

Many thanks to:
Carrie Greno, Seung Kim, Sean Ramirez, Shane Scanlan, Jeannie Harmon, Gayle Wise, Nicole Beebe, Helen Harrison, and all at Cook Communications, *and most of all, Mom.*

Go to the ant, . . .
consider its ways and be wise!
It has no commander,
no overseer or ruler,
yet it stores its provisions in summer
and gathers its food at harvest.
Proverbs 6:6–8

Each year in the forest bugs hold an event—
A dinner so massive that much time is spent
Hunting and gathering food from the woods,
And cooking a feast from their bountiful goods.

But one little ant always lagged far behind,
Never able to carry the food he could find.
So when all of the bugs would begin their big hunt,
They needed no help from a little ant runt.

A spider saw Ant and wondered aloud,
"Why don't you get food with the rest of the crowd?"
"I can't," said the ant. "See the leaves on that twig?
At my size it's not wise to lift food quite that big."

8

"**H**mm," wondered Spider. "Have you ever tried?"
"I'll bet we could do it if we both grabbed a side!"
So they each took a hold of the big leaf in question,
Though the thought of hard work gave the ant indigestion.

With Spider in back, and the ant in the front,
The leaf quickly rose as they let out a grunt.
"Goodness," said Ant, "you are certainly strong!
There's no way I could lift this if you weren't along!"

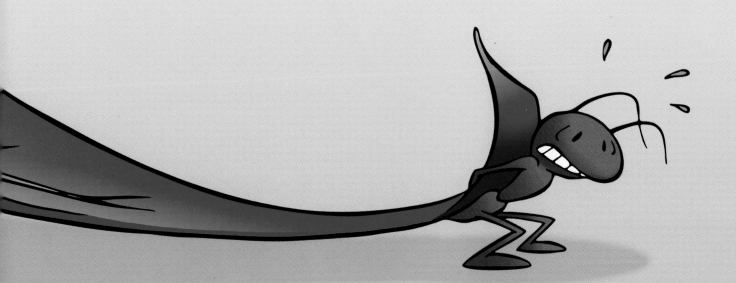

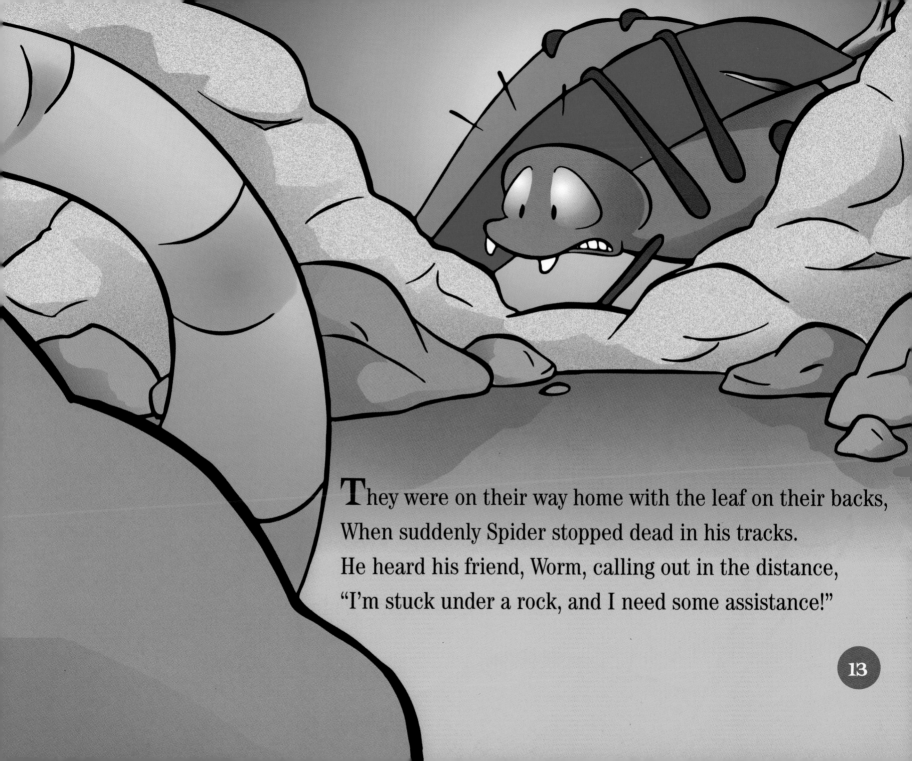

They were on their way home with the leaf on their backs,
When suddenly Spider stopped dead in his tracks.
He heard his friend, Worm, calling out in the distance,
"I'm stuck under a rock, and I need some assistance!"

Spider dashed to help Worm wriggle free from the stone,
Leaving Ant unaware he'd been left all alone.
Ant lugged the large leaf all the way to his hill,
Assuming his pal was helping him still.

14

When the leaf was home
safely, the ant turned around

And said loudly, with Spider
nowhere to be found,

"He must have just left
'cause his schedule's so tight.

I'll be certain to thank him
at dinner tonight!"

17

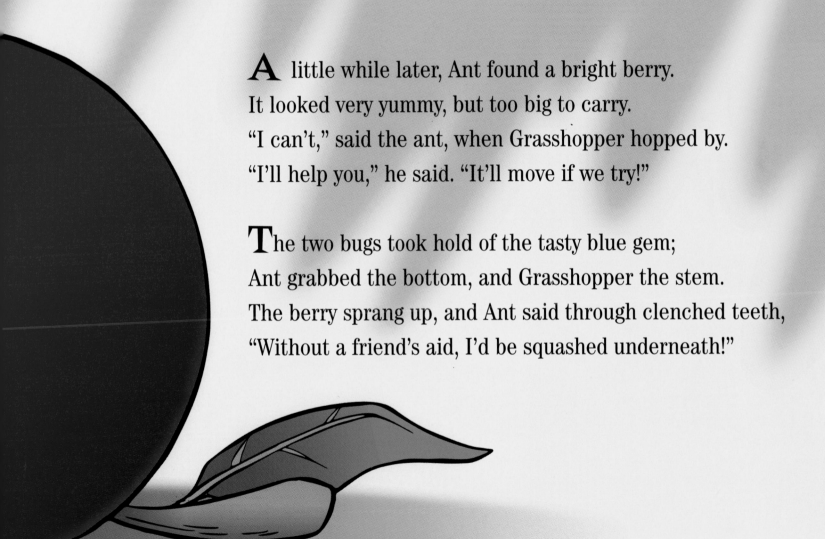

A little while later, Ant found a bright berry.
It looked very yummy, but too big to carry.
"I can't," said the ant, when Grasshopper hopped by.
"I'll help you," he said. "It'll move if we try!"

The two bugs took hold of the tasty blue gem;
Ant grabbed the bottom, and Grasshopper the stem.
The berry sprang up, and Ant said through clenched teeth,
"Without a friend's aid, I'd be squashed underneath!"

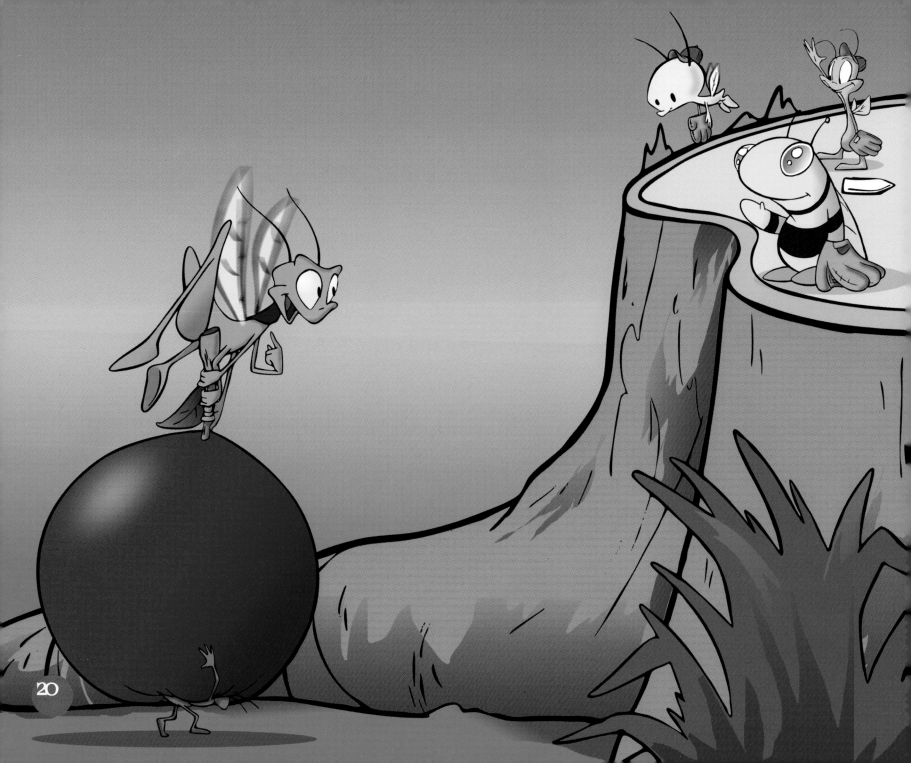

But Grasshopper stopped when he heard his friend's call,
"Hey! Put down that berry and come play baseball!"
So he hopped to his friends gathered there at home plate,
And Ant carried on, bearing all of the weight.

Ant marched home once again, put the fruit on the floor,
And said when he found his friend with him no more,
"When we finished the job, he leaped out of sight.
I'll be certain to thank him at dinner tonight!"

Party time came, and the ant couldn't wait,
So proud of the great mound of food on his plate.
He knew he must thank those who helped him the most,
So he quickly got up and then offered a toast.

24

"Thanks, Mister Spider," he started to say,
"For lending me two of your eight hands today.
And Grasshopper, thanks for a job quite well done.
You helped when my burden seemed over a ton!"

Spider stood up and then had to admit
He'd helped just a little and then had to split.
"I rescued the worm after hearing his groan.
You carried that leaf back all on your own!"

Then it was Grasshopper's turn to confess
His shock when he learned about Ant's big success.
"I started to help, but then left to play ball,
But you kept on going without slowing at all!"

This all came to Ant as quite a surprise.
He thought he was worthless because of his size.
Then Beetle jumped up and yelled, "Three cheers for Ant!
He can now say, 'I can!' instead of 'I can't!'"

A gigantic smile filled the ant's tiny face,
And every last bug in the whole party place
Picked up the ant who could now move small boulders
And whisked him away on the top of their shoulders.

"I can do everything through him who gives me strength."

Philippians 4:13 (NIV)

The Gigantic Little Hero

Ages: 4-7

My child's need:
To know that God will supply the strength we need for any task if
we will persevere until it is completed.

Spiritual Building Block:

Perseverance

Learning Styles

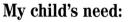

Sight: After you have read this story several times to your child, let him or her tell you the story from the illustrations. You could take on the role of the grasshopper or spider to add to the fun. When you are finished, pray with your child, thanking God for His ever-present help when we need Him.

Sound: After reading this story, talk with your child about times when he or she had a task that seemed too hard to do. Share suggestions of things you may have done when faced with similar circumstances. Memorize Philippians 4:13 together, and explain to your child that God is always there to help him or her when strength is needed to finish a task.

Touch: Children love to dramatize stories. Using this book as a script, let your child play the role of the ant. Use stuffed animals or siblings to play the parts of the grasshopper and spider. Videotape the performance to show other family members at a later time.